SOMEONE I LOVE HAS ALZHEIMER'S

Deborah Howard, RN, CHPN,
and Judy Howe, BA, MA

Consulting Editor: Dr. Paul Tautges

© 2012 Deborah Howard and Judy Howe

ISBN
Paper: 978-1-63342-063-2
epub: 978-1-63342-064-9
Kindle: 978-1-63342-065-6

Shepherd Press
P.O. Box 24
Wapwallopen, PA 18660

www.shepherdpress.com

All Scripture quotations, unless otherwise noted, are from The Holy Bible, English Standard Version. Copyright © 2001 by Crossway Bibles, a division of Good News Publishers.

All rights reserved.

First printed by Day One Publications

No part of this publication may be reproduced, or stored in a retrieval system, or transmitted, in any form or by any means, mechanical, electronic, photocopying, recording or otherwise, without the prior permission of Shepherd Press.

Designed by **documen**

Contents

	Introduction	4
1	Let Me Walk with You	6
2	Knowledge Is Power	12
3	"How Can I Help You?"	26
4	When I Am Afraid, I Will Trust God	51
	Conclusion	59
	Personal Application Projects	61
	Where Can I Get More Help?	62

To our parents,
Joe and Glen Koon,
and W. D. "Buddy" and Floye Howe,
with appreciation for the love and encouragement
they've given us over the years

Introduction

Certain words can strike terror in our hearts. "Cancer," for instance. Or "death," "root canal," "amputate." Words have power.

One of the most feared phrases in our vocabulary is "Alzheimer's disease." This diagnosis has the power to leave us paralyzed with disbelief and dread, whether it relates to us or to someone we love.

Outside the perspective of God's perfect will, we are justified in fearing this condition. Even before the diagnosis, Alzheimer's disease has already begun to erode the personality, function, and intellect of its victims. Insidious in its progression, it robs people of their lives and dignity, leaving grief and agony in its wake.

I hate Alzheimer's disease.

Only *within* the perspective of God's will can we begin to make sense of it. Our perception improves when we view this disease through a spiritual lens. No, dementia sufferers can't rise above dementia by the power of their wills. No, there is nothing the family can do to "make it all go away." But yes, we *can* find peace, joy, abiding love, and even humor along the journey.

I pray that these pages will serve to inform, encourage, and comfort you if someone you love has received this dreaded diagnosis.

1
Let Me Walk with You

This book approaches Alzheimer's disease from three perspectives: the physiological (theory and treatment), the practical (helpful suggestions for caregivers), and the spiritual (meditations upon God's goodness in the face of adversity). Professional and personal experience motivates my desire to help in any way I can.

A Page from My Own Story

My life and the lives of my family were forever changed in 1963 when my father was diagnosed with two brain tumors. The surgery to remove them left him severely impaired. My bright, robust, funny, talented, good-looking, gregarious father now had to be led to a chair, where he simply sat, staring. A knitted cap covered his healing scars.

The scars on the inside, however, proved harder to heal. Yet, incredibly, he regained more function than the doctors predicted. Though legally blind, some of his vision returned. Though halting in his movements, he was able to again walk unassisted. Though the notes on the musical score were blurry and elusive, he was able to return to his band room as the much-loved director he'd been before the surgery.

Understanding that Daddy would never be exactly as he was before, we did return to some semblance of normalcy. My mother became the reluctant head of the household, rising to every challenge. She was such a trooper that we never realized her heart was broken. We were just happy to have Daddy home. We didn't understand that, in a way, Mom had lost the husband of her dreams and that her heart was filled with fear, grief, and sorrow as she bravely struggled to care for him and her three children.

Daddy's decline continued, however. His field of vision diminished until he could see only a pinpoint, and even that was blurred by double vision. This vision loss decreased his overall function. But the truly damaging change was in his thinking.

Dementia increasingly undermined his mental capacity—and his pizzazz. The ongoing atrophy of his brain (along with the original damage from the surgeries) is thought to be the cause of his dementia. Though he doesn't have Alzheimer's disease, his dementia has been devastating nonetheless. By God's grace, I don't think he realizes it, even now. As we have watched him slowly fade away, he remains happy and sweet, appreciative and loving. He couldn't tell what day it is if his life depended on it. Yet he still loves his children and adores his wife. And for the past five decades, she's continued to care for him—lovingly, capably, and continuously.

A few years ago, however, we started noticing changes in Mom's personality, level of function, and ability to maintain the household. Concerned, I took her to the doctor, where she was eventually diagnosed with the early stages of Alzheimer's disease. My brother and I realized that our parents could not continue living by themselves and we had to make some difficult decisions regarding their welfare.

For our family, the solution was assisted living, where Mom still looks after Daddy. It's her shoulder he holds onto to walk to the dining room. She's his faithful advocate. She's the one who's there, twenty-four hours a day, to either listen to him repeat the same words, questions, or phrases, or to cope with the silence of a husband so mentally locked-in that he doesn't speak for hours.

For almost as long as I can remember, Daddy's been this way. And for as long as I can remember, my mom's been able to handle anything! So it's harder to respond to her loss of function than it has been with Daddy.

Why am I telling you this? Because it's important for you to know that I do not write from an untouched, academic viewpoint. I'm writing this book as a person whose life has been dramatically altered by this disease for decades.

Suffering Is Biblical

For Christians, our joy in Christ is not dependent upon a happy, trouble-free life. In fact, God's Word warns us that our lives *will* be touched by suffering, trials, and tribulations.

For instance, in John 16:33 Christ says,

> *In the world you will have tribulation. But take heart; I have overcome the world.*

The victory already belongs to him ... and to us.

Repeatedly, he assures us that our reward and ultimate joy do not reside in this world, but in the next. John 14:1-4 explains that Christ has gone ahead of us, to prepare a place for us where we will dwell with him forever. He is our refuge, our joy, our resting place. It is in the shadow of his sheltering wings that we will find ultimate peace, safety, and joy. In heaven, there will be no tears, no sorrow, no pain, no suffering—and no dementia.

But we're obviously not in heaven now. Therefore, we need to learn not how to *escape* from suffering and pain, but how to honor God in the midst of it.

We know this is possible because of the apostle Paul's remarkable example. His life as a believer was far from idyllic. He suffered multiple floggings, beatings, shipwrecks, hunger and thirst, imprisonments and persecution. Yet Paul was the one who said,

> *For I have learned in whatever situation*
> *I am to be content. I know how to be*
> *brought low, and I know how to abound.*
> *In any and every circumstance, I have*
> *learned the secret of facing plenty and*
> *hunger, abundance and need. I can do all*
> *things through him who strengthens me.*
> *(Philippians 4:11-13)*

Developing and maintaining this godly

perspective helps us persevere through the trials of Alzheimer's disease—or *any* adversity. The same God who strengthened Paul in every circumstance stands ready to do the same for us. His presence is the only cure for anything that ails us—even Alzheimer's disease. He may not take away the condition, but he'll see us through the experience. If we learn to keep our eyes focused upon him, we can travel this journey with faith, joy, love ... and hope.

2

Knowledge Is Power

One of the most effective ways of coping with adversity is education. Knowledge really is power! It provides the foundation to attack our problems, bolstering us with the assurance that we're doing all we can to bring calm, sensible management, and comfort to the situation. So, the more we understand about our adversary, Alzheimer's disease, the better we'll be able to predict what's coming and respond appropriately when it comes. Learning everything you can about Alzheimer's disease will make you more effective in caring for your loved one.

The fact that you're reading this book indicates that you're already on this positive, constructive path of learning about Alzheimer's disease. I hope to improve your understanding in the following pages.

What Is Alzheimer's Disease?

Dementia is a condition which causes changes in mental function. It affects thinking, reasoning, memory, personality, mood, and behavior. Almost everyone experiences memory impairment with age, but those with dementia experience losses severe enough to interfere with *the ability to function in life.*

Alzheimer's disease, frequently referred to as AD, is the most common form of dementia, but there are more than fifty others. For the purpose of this book, I will refer to all dementias as Alzheimer's disease, since the practical solutions and guidelines are similar, regardless of the diagnosis.

Some people are reluctant to seek medical advice when they suspect a problem in their thinking processes—afraid to discover that they have Alzheimer's disease. But it's very important to understand that many other medical problems, *some reversible*, can cause symptoms of dementia. These other conditions include meningitis, Lyme disease, metabolic problems, medication interactions, exposure to heavy metals or pesticides, alcohol abuse, and hypoxia (a state of oxygen deficiency). Sometimes, mental disorders,

Help! Someone I Love Has Alzheimer's

such as bipolar disorder or schizophrenia, can cause symptoms that respond well to medication. There's no specific test for AD, so the diagnosis is generally made by ruling out other causes and interpreting scores from cognitive evaluations (measurements of the mind's ability to think, perceive, and know). That's why I urge you to seek medical attention if you suspect a problem with your loved one.

But back to our original question: What is Alzheimer's disease? *It is a brain disorder resulting in a progressive decline in intellectual and social skills, interfering with a patient's ability to perform the activities of daily life and to interact meaningfully with others.*

It is more than simple forgetfulness, which is considered a normal characteristic of aging. AD symptoms are much more severe and incapacitating. The most likely cause for the vast majority of sufferers consists of aging, lifestyle, and/or environmental factors.

Although the causes of Alzheimer's are not definitive, its effect on the brain is well known and devastating. Alzheimer's disease kills brain cells and disables the connections between the remaining cells. When doctors examine the brain of an AD sufferer after death, they find that it is significantly smaller than a normal brain, and displays the two hallmarks of AD: *plaques*—protein clumps thought to kill brain cells and interfere with cell-to-cell communication in the brain; and *tangles*—abnormal fibers of protein in the brain which do not function properly; they can't carry nutrients and other essential materials to brain cells like normal fibers.

Warning Signs of Alzheimer's Disease

So when is the problem a result of normal aging and forgetfulness, and when is it time to see your doctor? The following are ten warning signs provided by the Alzheimer's Association:

» *Memory loss that disrupts daily life.* One of the most common signs of AD is memory loss, especially forgetting recently learned information. Others include forgetting important dates or events; asking for the same information over and over; and relying on memory aids or family members for things they used to handle on their own.

» *Challenges in planning or solving problems.* Some people may experience changes in their ability to develop and follow a plan or work with numbers. They may have trouble following a familiar recipe or keeping track of monthly bills. They may have difficulty concentrating and take much longer to do things than they did before.

» *Difficulty completing familiar tasks at home, at work, or at leisure.* People with AD often find it hard to complete daily tasks. They may have trouble driving to a familiar location, managing a budget at work, or remembering the rules of a favorite game.

» *Confusion with time or place.* People with AD can lose track of dates, seasons, and the passage of time. They may have trouble understanding something if it is not happening immediately. Sometimes they forget where they are or how they got there.

» *Trouble understanding visual images and spatial relationships.* For some people, having vision problems is a sign of AD. They may have difficulty reading, judging distances, and determining color or contrast. In terms of perception, they may pass a mirror and think that others are in the room, not realizing that they are the ones in the mirror.

» *New problems with words in speaking or*

writing. People with Alzheimer's may have trouble following or joining a conversation. They may stop in the middle of a conversation and have no idea how to continue, or they may repeat themselves. They may struggle with vocabulary, have problems finding the right word, or call things by the wrong name.

» *Misplacing things and losing the ability to retrace steps.* People with AD may put things in unusual places. They may lose things and be unable to go back over their steps to find them again. Sometimes they accuse others of stealing. This may occur more frequently over time.

» *Decreased or poor judgment.* People with AD may experience changes in judgment or decision-making. For example, they may use poor judgment when dealing with money, giving large amounts to telemarketers. They may pay less attention to grooming or keeping themselves clean.

» *Withdrawal from work or social activities.* Those with AD may start to remove themselves from hobbies, social activities, work projects, or sports. They may have trouble keeping up with a favorite sports team or remembering how to complete a favorite hobby. They may also avoid being social because of the changes they have experienced.

» *Changes in mood and personality.* The mood and personalities of people with AD can change. They can become confused, suspicious, depressed, fearful, or anxious. They may be easily upset at home, at work, with friends, or in places where they are out of their comfort zones.[1]

If your loved one exhibits any of these behaviors, it's time to seek a medical evaluation and diagnosis.

Diagnosis

In diagnosing AD, the doctor should first conduct a thorough medical history and physical exam to rule out problems caused by other conditions or medications. He or she may then administer cognitive or mental-status testing, typically asking your loved one to perform a combination of the following:

» Draw a clock face depicting a specific time
» Name the current date and time

» Remember three words after several other exercises
» Name ten items in a given category, such as animals or fruits
» Count backwards from 100 by sevens
» Follow a multiple-step set of instructions

The doctor will probably perform a standard neurological evaluation to assess balance, reflexes, and sensory function. If there are signs of cognitive impairment without a clear cause, the doctor may want additional tests.

The first testing options are simple blood and urine tests. Another is a spinal tap. Your doctor may also order one or more brain imaging scans, such as CT, MRI or PET scans.

Historically, brain imaging has been used to rule out other causes of dementia, such as stroke or tumor, leaving AD as the "default" diagnosis when no other cause is detected. Clinical trials and ongoing research are underway that may lead to a more definitive diagnosis, earlier intervention, and the hope of reversing or slowing the progression of the disease.

Alzheimer's Stages: How the Disease Progresses

Though there are differences in the progression of disease for each sufferer, doctors generally refer to three stages of AD: Mild, Moderate, and Severe. This assists sufferers and their caregivers in understanding their current situation within the progression of Alzheimer's and what to expect next.

MILD ALZHEIMER'S DISEASE
In the early stages, sufferers exhibit the following symptoms:

- Short-term memory loss. They have trouble remembering recent events or new information and may ask the same question repeatedly.
- Difficulty with multi-step tasks, solving problems, and making sound judgments. Planning a meal or balancing a checkbook may be overwhelming. They may make poor financial decisions.
- Personality changes. They may seem withdrawn, or unusually "touchy" or short-fused. They may have shorter attention spans

and fail to finish what they begin.

» Greater difficulty organizing and expressing their thoughts; difficulty finding the right words.

» Getting lost, even in familiar places, and misplacing belongings.

Moderate Alzheimer's Disease

From this stage of AD, sufferers may no longer be able to live independently. They exhibit the following symptoms:

» More extensive memory loss; inability to recall fundamental parts of their personal history, such as their date of birth.

» Worsened judgment and increased confusion. They forget where they are, what day it is, or even the time of year. They frequently fail to distinguish their belongings from others'.

» Increased tendency to wander, or to complain that they want to go home when they are at home. Difficulty identifying friends and family.

» The need for assistance with activities of daily living. They may become incontinent, losing control of their urine or bowel movements.

» Noticeable changes in personality and behavior, sometimes becoming suspicious and agitated. They may accuse people of stealing from them, poisoning them, or conspiring against them. They may have visual and/or auditory hallucinations.

» Increased restlessness, especially in the evening and at night. They may have episodes when (without cause) they scream, moan, curse, bite, kick, punch, or act out sexually.

Severe Alzheimer's Disease

The final stage takes a profound toll on sufferers' physical capabilities and overall mobility. By this stage, they require around-the-clock care.

» Inability to communicate verbally. They may occasionally utter words or phrases, but cannot string more than six words together meaningfully. They may express themselves using gibberish, cursing, or sounds.

» Typically, the loss of facial expression, including the ability to smile.

- » Increased difficulty swallowing. Decreased appetite.
- » Inability to perform *any* tasks of daily living.
- » Inability to walk unassisted. Muscles become rigid; reflexes become abnormal.
- » Incontinence in bowel and bladder.
- » Social withdrawal and isolation. They may not recognize even their closest friends or family.

For end-stage dementia sufferers, death usually occurs from complications associated with AD—aspiration (inhaling food or fluid into the lungs), falls, pneumonia, or other infections.

Treatment

Medications can treat the cognitive symptoms of AD by slowing the progression of the disease, especially if treatment begins at the earliest stage. Doctors may also prescribe medications to treat symptoms associated with Alzheimer's, such as depression, agitation, psychosis, and sleeplessness.

Along with medication, other therapies can sometimes benefit the AD sufferer. These include exercise, proper nutrition, a regular routine, sensory therapy, and a safe, comfortable environment.

Many people are interested in natural or alternative medicines. Unfortunately, there is little evidence to support claims of benefits from supplements such as Vitamins B, C, or E, beta carotene, folic acid, gingko, or Huperzine A (which should never be taken with other AD drugs). A recent panel of experts from the National Institute of Health cited the omega-3 fatty acids in fish oil as the *only* supplement with *potentially* beneficial effects on mental clarity.

Outlook

I wish I could offer an optimistic outlook for those afflicted with Alzheimer's, but I can't. The prognosis is poor and the ultimate outcome is death.

However, lest you think this applies only to Alzheimer's, remember that other diseases have the same trajectory (end-stage illnesses, organ failures, etc.). When someone you love is dying, regardless of the cause, you share a common experience with others. You're not alone in your suffering.

The most positive outlook I can offer is that Alzheimer's disease *can* be managed successfully.

Sufferers need not spend their remaining years in misery. With the support of family, friends, and experienced caregivers, patients can still experience love, comfort, and safety until the very end.

The Long Goodbye

I've heard this disease aptly called "The Long Goodbye." We bid farewell to our loved ones in stages. By the initial diagnosis, there has already been a loss of mental acuity. The next weeks and months cause mounting pain as we say goodbye to increasingly key characteristics of the ones we love. Little by little, they drift away, until they are mere shells of who they once were—shells that once housed those we loved, and those who loved us. Usually these dear ones die peacefully in their sleep. From beginning to end, this long goodbye may take months or years.

I don't say this to discourage you, but to *en*courage you to take the time now to enjoy your loved one as much as you can. Love him or her. Enjoy times of talking and laughing together. Let this special person know how much he or she means to you, what a difference he or she has made in your life, and that he or she won't be forgotten.

Encourage others to take the opportunity to express their feelings before it's too late. Soon, if not already, you will *be* your loved one's past—the repository for his or her memories. Help your loved one remember the past as you guide him or her along this final journey.

3
"How Can I Help You?"

Most of us assume that people think reasonably and logically—that we can appeal to those qualities in our communication with them. However, we must play by a new set of rules when a person loses the ability to think clearly.

My parents lived in a small, one-story home. Yet my father would stand up each evening and announce, "I'm going to go on upstairs." (He's never lived in a house with stairs.) My mother, attempting to help him think logically, would argue. "Joe, show me the stairs! Where do you see stairs?" Sometimes she'd lead him outside to the street and turn him to face the house. "Do you see an upstairs?"

My advice, which she eventually adopted, was to simply respond, "OK! I'll see you in the morning!" What difference did it make, as long as he easily found his bed and was happy, safe, and comfortable?

We try so hard to "win" conversations, arguments,

and disagreements, to defend and justify ourselves and to correct our loved ones. It's human nature. Yet you simply cannot do this with someone with Alzheimer's. If you continue to pursue these lines, it will result in frustration and confusion for both of you!

Take It Slow and Steady

Let's consider some of the new rules, with suggestions for caring for your loved one, maintaining your own sanity while doing so, and making the process as peaceful, calm, and manageable as possible. Caring for these precious people requires a multi-faceted approach, including medication, doctors' visits, proper nutrition, assistance with activities of daily living, exercise, a safe environment, and perhaps other or alternative therapies. Though I realize this sounds daunting, there are people and organizations which can help, such as friends and other family members, your local area agency on aging, Medicaid, hospice, Meals on Wheels, private caregivers, assisted living facilities, and nursing homes. Before discussing specific caregiving guidelines, I'd like to address some personal qualities that you, the caregiver, will find necessary.

Effective caregivers require three essential traits to successfully complete their mission with grace and composure: humility, patience, and a sense of humor.

HUMILITY

What does *humility* have to do with anything? It is essential because you cannot concern yourself with *winning* all the battles, as I mentioned above. Humility helps you allow your loved one to win—even if he or she is wrong and you're right.

Judy Howe and I have been friends for almost forty years. We've supported each other as we have both strived to lovingly care for our parents. I've never known anyone who exemplified the quality of humility as much as Judy did with her father.

Since she has contributed so much to researching and writing this book, I've asked her to share a little of her experience here.

JUDY'S STORY

As my father's primary caregiver for his last few years, I can speak about dementia from a personal perspective. My father's cognitive and physical decline spanned many years.

Buddy Howe was an intelligent, charming, athletically gifted young man. After serving in the Army Air Corps in World War II, he was awarded the Soldier's Medal, the highest honor awarded for an act of valor in a non-combat situation, for running *into* a burning plane to rescue the crew.

After the war he went into business for himself as a building contractor. For decades, at work and at home, he was "The Boss." However, in his sixties, his body and mind began to betray him.

By the time he was eighty, physical infirmities left him in constant pain, with limited vision and hearing, a weak heart, shortness of breath, contrary limbs, and numbness in his hands and feet. A series of strokes destroyed his short-term memory. Though he could charmingly engage in superficial conversations, he was unable to remember them. Multiple strokes also caused many of the common dementia symptoms that are so frustrating to caregivers: agitation, irritability, paranoia, and a hair-trigger temper.

Unlike Deborah's father, Daddy was aware of his limitations, and he didn't like them one bit. I have to say that my father went down fighting. Unfortunately, much of the time he was fighting *us*!

My mother never quite accepted the idea that discord was to be avoided at all costs. I think she found it hard to believe that Daddy was beyond being reasoned with and being *made* to remember. She seemed to think she just needed to try harder. But the harder she tried, the more his agitation mounted, and the more pronounced his symptoms became.

In contrast, I learned to adopt the role of scapegoat for *everything*. I found that if I promptly assumed guilt and apologized, Daddy was almost always willing to "forgive me" and move on. I realize that this can be hard to do when you know you've done nothing wrong. But it certainly helps avoid frustration and turmoil if you can!

For instance, many times he accused me of failing to tell him about a doctor's appointment and springing it upon him at the last moment. No matter how many times I had told him about the appointment, I'd simply say, "Oh, I'm so sorry. I thought I'd told you. I'll try to remember next time."

If he knocked something over, I'd rush to right it, and instead of his becoming frustrated, I'd quickly volunteer, "I'm so sorry I left that there!" In both of these situations, there was no further hassle. No more frustration. He accepted my apology and we moved on.

My father was a fiercely independent man who had spent most of his life being *in charge*. In the end, he had to depend on someone to provide assistance with all the activities of daily living.

Although it sometimes seemed that nothing I did pleased him, I knew it was the disease talking, not my father. I didn't take it *personally*. That may be another of the most difficult and most important messages I have for caregivers—don't take it personally when your loved one lashes out. Typically, you are simply the safest target for his or her anger and frustration.

We did everything we could to make the end of my father's life as comfortable and dignified as possible. He was a hero in our eyes, as well as in the eyes of our country. We believed he should be treated with respect and consideration. In his final days, we realized that he needed more help than we could provide, so we transferred him to an inpatient hospice facility. We took turns staying there with him.

Let me affirm what Deborah said above about encouraging others to express their feelings before it's too late. By doing just that, my cousin, Bobby, earned a special place in my father's heart—and in mine.

They had always been close. So when Bobby walked into the hospice room, Daddy's face lit up like a child's on Christmas morning. Bobby told my father one last time how much he cared for him, expressing his gratitude for Daddy's positive influence. They talked and laughed for about fifteen minutes before Daddy dozed off, never to have another lucid conversation.

In the end, he *did* go gently into the night, drifting away in his sleep as my sister kept watch.

As Judy mentioned, people with AD will not remember that you have told them *repeatedly* that they have a doctor's appointment today. Nothing you say, no amount of scene-setting, reminders, or witnesses, will *ever* help them remember. For them, *it didn't happen*. Instead, they feel you are conspiring against them, and they become paranoid.

If, like my well-meaning mom, you take them outside and show them "No upstairs!" it won't mean anything to them. *You can never win.* Not, that is, if your objective is to *make* them remember or understand and, thus, *be right*!

First Peter 5:5 says,

> *Clothe yourselves, all of you, with humility toward one another, for "God opposes the proud but gives grace to the humble."*

God also gives us grace to *be* humble. Humility should characterize our lives at all times, but rarely are we challenged more than when dealing with dementia sufferers. When your loved one's memory or reason fails, your best approach is to agree or immediately apologize for *your* failure and assume blame.

Swallowing your pride is hard. However, I have witnessed situations that turned into shouting matches because the caregivers were determined to prove themselves right instead of accepting the "blame" and moving on peacefully.

Patience

The next essential trait is *patience*. Many times you'll be forced to repeat things over and over, or listen to your loved one relate the same stories, the same comments, the same objections, again and again. Plus, if you take things at the sufferer's pace, you will be required to wait for him or her to do in minutes what you could do in seconds. While your loved one struggles to find the right word, you'll want to blurt it out instead of waiting.

You *must* cultivate patience if you are to continually repeat yourself without adding, "... like I've already told you 500 times!" Even without the words, if your tone of voice is impatient, your loved one will probably perceive it and tempers may flare, setting off worsened AD symptoms.

Certainly you can assist your loved one by trying to supply the right word or helping to finish a thought, or by stepping in to assist with a task that has him or her stymied. But be wary of jumping in *before* help is wanted: you may trigger irritation or anger.

Many AD patients, especially in the early stages, are aware of their losses. Give them the time they need to mourn those losses, realizing that they are feeling at least *some* denial and anger. Be patient and kind with them.

Like humility, patience is a Christian virtue that should characterize our lives. Romans 12:12 says,

> *Rejoice in hope, be patient in tribulation,*
> *be constant in prayer.*

AD is the kind of tribulation that absolutely requires patience.

If patience isn't your strong suit, take heart. As it is part of the fruit of the Spirit (Galatians 5:22-23), we know that it is spiritually supplied. Ask the Lord to grant you patience as you struggle through this experience. It is a virtue that *can be learned*. It will take prayer and focused energy, but it will get easier as you go along.

Start with baby steps. While waiting at a red light or in a long line at the supermarket, practice being patient. Take a deep breath. Enjoy

Help! Someone I Love Has Alzheimer's

something in your surroundings. Pray. Smile at someone. Remind yourself that, Lord willing, the important errand you're on *will* be accomplished, even if not as quickly as you'd hoped.

In 1 Thessalonians 5:14 we read,

> And we urge you, brothers, admonish the idle, encourage the fainthearted, help the weak, be patient with them all.

Certainly these dear sufferers of AD can be considered "the weak" and many times they can become fainthearted. So we *must* be patient.

A Sense of Humor

The third essential element in caring for someone with Alzheimer's disease is *a sense of humor*; it will help the sufferer *and the caregiver* through this extended goodbye. For as long as possible, and as much as possible, laugh *with* your loved one. While anger worsens AD symptoms, laughter seems to alleviate them, if only briefly.

For instance, my mom recently decided she needed a motorized scooter. But what she told her doctor was, "I'm ready for an electric chair!" When the doctor and I giggled, I said, "I think you mean a power chair, not an electric chair." Realizing what she'd said, she laughed along with us.

When your loved one reaches the later stages of the disease, it is especially important that you have a trusted confidant. It's better to laugh than to cry, and often those will seem to be your only options. Although it requires putting distance between yourself and the situation, viewing your circumstances through the essential lens of humor can provide some much-needed relief from stress.

Therefore, show humility, exercise patience, and express a sense of humor. These will pay great dividends as you care for your loved one, and will make the experience less stressful and more enjoyable for both of you.

The Nitty-Gritty: Practical Guidelines for Caregiving

Legal Preparedness

Before we address the physical care of your loved one, I need to say a word about the financial aspect of care. The first step in planning how to pay for your loved one's future medical and living expenses is to make a careful analysis of his or her present financial situation. Let me encourage you, therefore, to seek the counsel of an attorney, social worker, or financial adviser as soon as possible after an AD diagnosis.

A careful, responsible financial plan may include:

» A will, outlining your loved one's final wishes and determining distributions of property after death
» A durable power of attorney, authorizing someone to make legal and medical decisions when your loved one is no longer competent
» A living will, describing your loved one's wishes regarding the use of artificial life-support systems
» A living trust, especially if the estate has significant worth

Assist your loved one, if necessary, in organizing policies, accounts, and assets. Make sure that two people know where these records are stored.

I believe that one of the greatest gifts your loved one can give *you*, the caregiver, is his or her funeral pre-arrangement. If your loved one has already progressed beyond this ability, I urge you to take this step for him or her. It will be far easier and less emotionally pressured to do it early in the process than to wait until after your loved one's death.

Grief sometimes clouds decision-making.

One final note before we leave legal issues: automobile liability. For most people, cars represent independence and freedom. Taking your loved one's keys deprives him or her of both. It would be nice if people offered up their keys voluntarily, yet that seldom happens. Though this is a difficult, emotionally charged issue, it is imperative that you take a strong stand. Allowing a person with AD to drive is dangerous for the driver, passengers, and others on the road. Enlist your loved one's doctor or closest friends and family to help in this delicate, but critical, matter.

Medication

Medication is, of course, the purview of your doctor. As the caregiver, however, you have responsibilities too. Initially, your loved one may be able to take the medications appropriately with the use of a pill box. I prepared my parents' boxes weekly and my mother gave the meds as scheduled. It was when she developed problems using the pill box correctly that I knew she needed assisted living.

You need to maintain a complete list of your loved one's medications, including over-the-counter drugs and supplements. For each medication, you

Help! Someone I Love Has Alzheimer's

should note the following information:

- » Medication name
- » Dosage (drug strength and number of pills taken)
- » Time it's due to be given
- » Who prescribed it and for what condition or purpose

Keep this list updated and take it with you to all doctors' appointments, or simply take all the medications with you.

Doctors' Visits

Alzheimer's sufferers cannot recall their symptoms dependably. Some won't mind if you supply the information for them. Others may feel that you are treating them like children and may become angry or uncooperative. One thing I have found helpful is to ask for a note to be put on the sufferer's medical chart, indicating that he or she has Alzheimer's.

You may find it helpful to supply needed information in writing and give it to the doctor. However, sometimes your only choice is to speak the truth in your loved one's presence, knowing that it may sting in the short term, but that it will be quickly forgotten.

If you *can* speak freely during the exam, having careful notes available may prove useful. If your loved one starts showing a new symptom, for example, instead of relying on your memory, jot down the date you first noticed the symptom. You may think that you won't forget when it started, but by the time you see the doctor, it might be difficult to recall the exact sequence of events.

Another piece of advice: doctors are usually in a hurry. But don't forget that they work for you! It's important that you don't leave the doctor's office more confused than when you arrived. Before the doctor leaves the room, make sure you understand what he or she has told you about your loved one's condition, about any changes in medication, or changes to daily protocols. (The Mayo Clinic Web site has in-depth information on preparing for doctors' visits; see the section "Where Can I Get More Help?" at the end of this book.)

NUTRITION

Nutrition is a vital part of the AD sufferer's therapy; at the same time, it is a very personal issue and must be adjusted to the individual and the disease stage. People with dementia may forget to eat or drink or may become extremely picky about their food. They are particularly prone to dehydration. They should be encouraged, but not forced, to eat a balanced, healthy diet accompanied by plenty of liquids. What I recommend is small, frequent meals or snacks rather than three large meals.

As the disease progresses, sufferers lose their appetite as well as the focused energy to eat. When this occurs, your loved one may tolerate cool food rather than hot, bland rather than spicy, and soft rather than chewy—you want to aim for decreasing the energy required for eating. I recommend cooked cereals, soft scrambled eggs, Popsicles (cut into bite-sized pieces), Jell-O, ice cream, mashed potatoes, and shakes made from ice cream and a nutritional supplement (e.g., Ensure, Glucerna, Boost, Instant Breakfast).

One of the most common problems is constipation. One tip I've learned is to offer sufferers a small glass of prune juice mixed with Sprite every evening. This seems to work as well as any laxative on the market, while providing nutritional value and hydration. It also seems to go down a little easier when accompanied by a cookie or two!

Eventually, your loved one will lose all desire for

food. This may be the body's natural response to the end of life. Many well-intentioned caregivers and doctors rush to place feeding tubes in these patients. This crossroads will require tough decisions. It's time to decide whether to let nature take its course or to intervene in terms of artificial nutrition. A living will usually outlines how far one wishes to go with "heroics" at the end of life. Respect your loved one's choices. (For a more complete understanding of this vital issue, I urge you to read ch. 7 in my book *Sunsets: Reflections for Life's Final Journey*; see the section "Where Can I Get More Help?" at the end of this book.)

ACTIVITIES OF DAILY LIVING

Activities of Daily Living, or ADLs, cover a range of activities, from personal grooming and dressing to feeding oneself and using the toilet. In the early stages, Alzheimer's sufferers can follow verbal cues to perform these tasks. Later, they require minimal assistance, and eventually they become completely dependent on others to perform these tasks for them.

As noted above, one of the first signs of Alzheimer's disease is a lack of personal grooming. At this stage, sufferers may be unable to assess their degree of cleanliness or the state of their clothes. Beyond that, frequently they simply cannot plan the necessary steps required to bathe and dress.

For example, to help your father wash his face, you may need to drape a soapy washcloth over his hand and ask him to wash his face with it. Once he's finished, you'll need to take it back, rinse it, drape it over his hand again, and then ask him to rinse his face with it. Then you'll need to hand him a towel and instruct him to dry his face. You can't simply hand him a dry washcloth, a bar of soap, and a towel, and expect him to be able to perform the necessary steps to wash his face.

People with AD lose their ability to "sequence." An example is putting underwear on *over* their jeans instead of underneath. This lack of sequencing ability contributes to their grooming slips; even if they recognize the need, they can't master the process.

One goal of providing hygiene for your loved one is keeping him or her smelling nice. Many times the smell of urine is pervasive, even if you've used soap and water. Here's a little trick: use shaving cream to wash private parts. It thoroughly cleans and leaves a pleasant fragrance that masks urine smells.

In conclusion, it is important to let Alzheimer's sufferers participate in each activity as fully as possible. Once any task is completed, compliment your loved one on how well he or she did, without being effusive; it is important for sufferers to feel they've accomplished something, without feeling patronized.

Exercise
Encourage exercise within the boundaries of safety, comfort, and practicality. Exercise has cognitive benefits for all of us, including Alzheimer's sufferers. Exercise also helps lessen anxiety, improve mood, and make constructive use of time.

In addition, weight-bearing exercise, such as walking, tones muscles, preserves balance, and protects bone mass, reducing the risk of falls. It also improves appetite and helps ward off constipation. Check with your doctor before beginning an exercise program, and adjust your loved one's activities as the disease progresses.

The Environment
Alzheimer's sufferers need a safe, calm, regulated environment. Your first concern is to protect your loved one from falls. To do this:

Help! Someone I Love Has Alzheimer's

- » Install grab bars in showers, baths, and by the toilet
- » Place non-slip rugs on uncarpeted floors, especially kitchens and bathrooms
- » Clear clutter from pathways
- » Ensure proper lighting
- » When your loved one becomes unsteady, do not allow him or her to walk unassisted
- » Secure cords or cables along walls and out of walkways

Because dementia sufferers are easily overwhelmed, de-clutter the rooms in which your loved one spends the most time. Sorting through a cluttered visual field can be extremely confusing for him or her.

Another consideration is the auditory environment. Some of us leave the television on as "background noise." However, background noise can contribute to anxiety for Alzheimer's sufferers, especially when loud, annoying commercials suddenly jolt them from a light snooze, causing them to become nervous or agitated. To maximize communication, reduce background noise when speaking to your loved one.

People with Alzheimer's tend to become

withdrawn. Encourage socialization, but limit the number of visitors at any given time, and keep the visits brief. Avoid crowds, noisy environments, and unfamiliar places.

A final note on the environment: AD sufferers tend to wander. You may want to get double-cylinder deadbolt locks for exterior doors and keep the keys in a safe location. If wandering continues to be problematic, notify your local police department. They will help locate and return your loved one if they know about the situation.

OTHER THERAPIES

Sensory therapy, such as pet therapy, has proven effective with many sufferers. When a therapy dog is brought into the room, patients sitting listlessly in wheelchairs have been known to suddenly perk up and call to the dog, stroking it, and talking to it, even if they have stopped talking to people.

Other forms of sensory therapy, such as art or music, are also helpful for some. Music, in particular, seems to trigger memories—or at least a pleasant feeling of nostalgia—and helps sufferers connect with others, improving both their mood and their function. Playing music you and your loved one have enjoyed together can be especially gratifying. You may want to simply share memories with your loved one, perhaps looking through old photos or watching home movies.

Caring for Yourself

There is one other important factor we should discuss before moving on: YOU! Caregiver burnout is a significant problem. Most caregivers are stressed, sleep-deprived, and have put their own needs last on their "to do" list.

But whether your loved one acknowledges it or not, you are the most important person in the AD sufferer's life as he or she steadily becomes more impaired. Caring for yourself helps your loved one too!

An old Southern expression goes, "You can't give from a dry well." If you do not take the time to replenish your physical and spiritual energy, your effectiveness in caring for your loved one will decline. Your judgment will suffer. Your health will deteriorate.

It's important to give yourself breaks in caregiving. One way you can do this is very simple but rarely utilized—*ask someone for help!* Ask a friend or family member, a pastor, or church member to sit with your loved one long enough for you to run to the store, have your hair done, or go to a movie.

People always say, "If you need anything, just call." But how many caregivers do that? I advise you to make that call. Say, "I'd love to be able to take a long bath or sleep for two or three hours without worrying about Mama. Would you mind staying long enough for me to do that?" Or say, "Come to think of it, could you pick up a few things for me from the grocery store?" People generally want to help but don't know *how*. Teach them by making specific requests.

Most importantly, don't allow your spiritual well-being to fall victim to your preoccupation with providing excellent care. Matthew 6:33 says,

> *Seek first the kingdom of God and his righteousness, and all these things will be added to you.*

God promises to supply our needs if we continue to seek him. Even when it seems that every minute of every day is spoken for, we *must* find time to seek God. Caring for your loved one is a noble, honorable undertaking. But *never* are we to place anything or anyone above the Lord in our attentions or our affections.

The apostle Paul asked the Lord to remove a specific problem on three occasions. Each time the

Lord had the same answer:

> *My grace is sufficient for you, for my power is made perfect in weakness.*
> (2 Corinthians 12:9)

God's grace is sufficient for us as well. No, we may not be able to continue to give through our own strength, but we can persevere to the end through *his un*limited strength and grace.

Replenishing your energy and spirit is accomplished in different ways for different people. For me, nothing is as satisfying as my quiet time on the back porch, meditating upon the beauty of nature and the glory of God. Bible study and prayer keep my mind tuned to God and my heart peaceful. I urge you to make time for this.

However, you may find solace and refreshment in other ways too: taking a walk, reading a book, scheduling a spa day, lunching with a friend. However you choose to replenish your spirit and energize your body, I cannot urge you strongly enough to *do it*. As a caregiver, you'll be called upon to give from that well for a long time. Make sure you have an inexhaustible supply of energy by taking time to replenish it.

4
When I Am Afraid, I Will Trust God

No one wants to have Alzheimer's disease. Some might think it's not fair for anyone to suffer such a debilitating illness ... or *any* illness, for that matter. For Christians, it comes down to a basic question when anything this heartbreaking comes their way: "Where is God in all of this?"

That's what we must reconcile. If God is sovereign (the Supreme Ruler, Lord, Master) over all things, as the Bible teaches, doesn't that mean that he is sovereign over anything that comes into our lives? Doesn't that mean that he decides who gets what and when? We're taught that God loves his children and that he is totally good. So, if that is true, how could he send grief our way? That may not seem like love to you.

God's Sovereignty, Justice, and Goodness

In a book this size, there's no way to deal exhaustively with such a weighty question. But it's

Help! Someone I Love Has Alzheimer's

not so complex that we cannot address it in a brief but coherent way. (See also some of the books in the "Where Can I Get More Help?" section.)

Let's set down some basic truths.

» God is completely and totally all-powerful, trustworthy, just, holy, and omniscient (Genesis 18:25b; 2 Chronicles 20:6; Mark 10:27; Hebrews 13:5).

» God is sovereign over all things, including illness (Nehemiah 9:6; Isaiah 46:9-11; Colossians 1:16-17).

» God is sovereign over life and death (Ecclesiastes 3:2a; Acts 17:25).

» God is sovereign over the time we are born—and the time we die. Neither comes one moment before or after his ordained time for us (Job 14:5; Psalm 139:16; Ecclesiastes 8:8).

» God promises to love us unconditionally in Christ. He doesn't love us less when we're "bad" than when we're "good" (Romans 5:8).

» God is faithful in keeping his promises (Psalm 145:13b; Hebrews 6:18).

» God's ways and thoughts are higher than

ours. We cannot comprehend his reasoning or impugn his judgments (Isaiah 40:13-14; Romans 9:20-21; Romans 11:33-34; 1 Corinthians 1:25).

» God is the divine Master-Planner for all of life—including the infinitesimal part we fit into (Lamentations 3:38; Acts 17:26-28).

That being said, how can we reconcile the goodness of God with our pain and suffering? Several of these biblical truths come into consideration.

Our God is a God of means. He uses those means to accomplish his purposes. Alzheimer's disease is just another tool in his divine toolbox. Sometimes God afflicts those he loves because that particular tool is required to work his will into their lives. He brings what is needed to mold individuals into the people he has ordained them to be. Through these circumstances, he changes not only the individuals, but their friends and families as well.

My family's life has been altered significantly by my father's prolonged illness. Perhaps we are who we are today because of it. All I know is that Daddy's condition has a purpose, and that purpose was designed by a loving God.

Because of sin in this world, we know that we

will all die of something (unless the Lord returns first). There are no accidents in life. Sometimes a car crash is the means God uses to take us home; sometimes he uses natural disasters or violence; and sometimes he uses disease—natural causes. If he chooses to use Alzheimer's as his tool, how can we argue with him? His ways are higher than ours; his thoughts are loftier. We will never fully comprehend the wisdom of Almighty God.

Our responsibility is to humbly submit to *whatever* God has in store for us. We readily and enthusiastically accept his blessings. Though it's much more difficult, we should readily, humbly, and sweetly accept the trials he brings our way as well, knowing that they will always result in at least two things: ultimate good for us and glory for him!

Obedience to Our Master

My father has always been a man of warmth, joy, and integrity. Was it fair for God to afflict him as he has? You bet it was. My father belongs to him. God created him.

My dad has never complained about his lot in life and, to my knowledge, has never felt sorry for himself. Instead, he sees himself as someone who has received great blessings from the Lord. And he has!

God gave him great gifts—caring parents, salvation, talent, intelligence. God brought my mother into his life—providing him with someone who would love and care for him for the rest of his life. God brought three children into his life who surrounded him with love, respect, and admiration. Though my parents have never had a lot of money, God provided enough for them to survive and to raise their children. He will continue to provide for them until he calls them home.

Everyone who knows my father thinks the world of him, in part because of his sweet attitude in the face of adversity. No, God has not dealt unfairly with my father, but has richly blessed him—even through his infirmity.

Some might even wonder what makes him so special. I'll tell you. What makes my father remarkable is not who he is, or what he has done. It's the One he has faithfully believed in. My father is a child of the King. Our only true worth is in Christ's righteousness applied to our hearts.

God's Solution Is Jesus Christ

The cross of Christ is the ultimate solution to the problem of suffering and pain. On that cross, Jesus not only conquered sin and death, but he also entered into human suffering and can, therefore, sympathize with us in it. God, in his infinite grace, did not leave Christ on the cross, but raised him from the dead to reign with him forever. Christ's life, death, and resurrection secured the eternal salvation of all who will trust in him.

If he could, my father would urge you to know Jesus, and would tell you what that means. Salvation is not a matter of anything we can do to earn it, of any effort we can put forth, of any good thought or deed we could muster. Romans 9:16 says,

> So then it depends not on human will or exertion, but on God, who has mercy.

Our hearts are steeped in sin from birth. Without a Savior, we would all rush toward eternal destruction. So God, in his wisdom and lovingkindness, provided the only Sacrifice that could atone for our sins: Jesus Christ, his Son. Because God loves his children, he calls them to faith, to believe upon Jesus. As John 3:16 says,

> For God so loved the world, that he gave his only Son, that whoever believes in him should not perish but have eternal life.

When we believe in Christ, we are credited with his righteousness. Our salvation depends not on the good that *we* do, but upon the good that *Christ* did on our behalf. It is only through this that we are saved.

When we confess our sinful state before God and bow the knee to his Lordship in our lives, believing in him as our Savior, he promises to save us from destruction and bring us into his glorious light. He doesn't promise that we'll have rosy lives from then on. Instead, he promises that we will suffer—but that he will be with us in the midst of our suffering. Though he blesses us along the journey and gives us cause for great joy, he also sends hardship our way.

One such hardship is Alzheimer's disease. Slowly watching someone you love fade from existence is heart-rending. It tests the limits of our energy, patience, emotion, and faith. Let us not be found wanting. AD is a means to an end—an end that God has every right to bring. Let us demonstrate our love for God by adopting an attitude of sweet, humble submission to his will. Let us show others that we can live with joy and contentment in the midst of our trials, because we know what awaits us on the other side. Our deepest concerns will fade from existence once we come face to face with our Lord. So, in this life, "our truest happiness is perfect submission to God's will, and it is the highest charity to pray that all mankind may know it, obey it, and submit to it."[2] That is my prayer for you.

Conclusion

I hope the information in this book has increased your understanding of Alzheimer's disease and that the practical guidelines will assist you in caring for your loved one on the difficult journey you are embarking upon. Even more, I hope that the scriptural references and support they offer soothe your soul.

Caring for those struggling with Alzheimer's disease is demanding, frustrating, and challenging. It requires a sacrificial attitude that sometimes defies worldly reasoning. Yet there is never a time when our Lord is not there with us, in our midst, as we labor to care for our loved ones.

He supplies one essential element that propels us to persevere: hope! So I urge you to cling to that hope as you strive to overcome the evil of this fallen world. Let others see Christ in your godly, peaceful attitude in the midst of the trial known as Alzheimer's disease.

> May the God of hope fill you with all joy
> and peace in believing, so that by the
> power of the Holy Spirit you may abound
> in hope.
>
> (Romans 15:13)

Personal Application Projects

1. Alzheimer's disease is one of the difficulties God has brought into your life. Read 1 Corinthians 1:7b-9. How can you use this promise to encourage yourself as times get tough?

2. Read Matthew 25:34-40. How can you apply verse 40 to your motivation for caregiving when times get tough?

3. Read Galatians 6:2. What principle do you find in this verse that supports your desire to be a caregiver even during the hardest times?

4. We tend to focus on our own pain and heartache. What happens to our attitude when we think of others in the midst of our tough times? Read and meditate on Philippians 2:3-11. How is the humility of Jesus an example in th is regard?

5. Write down one encouraging passage of Scripture and memorize it so that you can easily quote it when times get tough.

Where Can I Get More Help?

BOOKS

Atkins, MD, Charles, *The Alzheimer's Answer Book: Professional Answers to More Than 250 Questions about Alzheimer's and Dementia* (Naperville, IL: Sourcebooks, Inc., 2008)

Broyles, Frank, *Coach Broyles' Playbook for Alzheimer's Caregivers: A Practical Tips Guide* (Fayetteville, AR: University of Arkansas Press, 2006)

DeBaggio, Thomas, *Losing My Mind: An Intimate Look at Life with Alzheimer's* (New York: Free Press, 2003)

Delehanty, Hugh, and Ginzler, Elinor, *Caring for Your Parents: The Complete Family Guide (AARP)* (New York: Sterling Publishing, 2008)

Howard, Deborah, *Sunsets: Reflections for Life's Final Journey* (Wheaton, IL: Crossway, 2005)
——*Where Is God in All of This?* (Phillipsburg, NJ: P&R, 2009)

Mack, Wayne A., *Down, But Not Out: How to Get Up When Life Knocks You Down* (Phillipsburg, NJ: P&R, 2005)

——and Howard, Deborah, *It's Not Fair! Finding Hope When Times Are Tough* (Phillipsburg, NJ: P&R, 2009)

McHugh, MD, Dr. Paul R., Mace, MA, Ms. Nancy L., and Rabins, MD, MPH, Dr. Peter V., *The 36-Hour Day: A Family Guide to Caring for Persons with Alzheimer's Disease, Related Dementing Illnesses, and Memory*

Loss in Later Life (Baltimore, MD: The Johns Hopkins University Press, 1999)

Owens, Virginia Stem, *Caring for Mother: A Daughter's Long Goodbye* (Louisville, KY: Westminster John Knox Press, 2007)

Web Sites

"Alzheimer's Disease Health Center" at WebMD, www.webmd.com

"Alzheimer's Disease" at Mayo Clinic, www.mayoclinic.com

Alzheimer's Association, www.alzheimersassociation.org

"Alzheimer's Information" at National Institute on Aging, www.nia.nih.gov/Alzheimers

Family Caregiver Alliance, www.caregiver.org

"Caregiving" at AARP, www.aarp.org

End Notes

1 Based on "10 Signs of Alzheimer's," Alzheimer's Association, at www.alz.org. Accessed September 2011.

2 J. C. Ryle, Ryle's *Expository Thoughts on the Gospels: St. Matthew* (Grand Rapids: Zondervan, [n.d.]), 52.

BOOKS IN THE HELP! SERIES INCLUDE...

Help! He's Struggling with Pornography
 ISBN 978-1-63342-003-8

Help! Someone I Love Has Been Abused
 ISBN 978-1-63342-006-9

Help! My Toddler Rules the House
 ISBN 978-1-63342-009-0

Help! Someone I Love Has Cancer
 ISBN 978-1-63342-012-0

Help! I Want to Change
 ISBN 978-1-63342-015-1

Help! My Spouse Has Been Unfaithful
 ISBN 978-1-63342-021-2

Help! I Have Breast Cancer
 ISBN 978-1-63342-024-3

Help! I'm a Slave to Food
 978-1-63342-027-4

Help! My Teen Struggles With Same-Sex Attractions
 ISBN 978-1-63342-030-4

Help! She's Struggling With Pornography
 ISBN 978-1-63342-033-5

Help! I Can't Get Motivated
 ISBN 978-1-63342-036-6

Help! I'm a Single Mom
 ISBN 978-1-63342-039-7

Help! I'm Confused About Dating
 ISBN 978-1-63342-042-7

Help! I'm Drowning in Debt
 ISBN 978-1-63342-045-8

Help! My Teen is Rebellious
 ISBN 978-1-63342-048-9

Help! I'm Depressed
 ISBN 978-1-63342-051-9

Help! I'm Living With Terminal Illness
 ISBN 978-1-63342-054-0

Help! I Feel Ashamed
 ISBN 978-1-63342-057-1

Help! I Want to Understand Submission
 ISBN 978-1-63342-060-1

Help! I Can't Handle All These Trials
 ISBN 978-1-63342-066-3

Help! I Can't Forgive
 ISBN 978-1-63342-069-4

Help! My Anger is Out of Control
 ISBN 978-1-63342-072-4

Help! My Friend is Suicidal
 ISBN 978-1-63342-075-5

Help! I'm in a Conflict
 ISBN 978-1-63342-078-6

Help! I Need a Church
 ISBN 978-1-63342-081-6

(More titles in preparation)